WITHDRAWN

Weekend Fun

Let's Go to a Park

By Mary Hill

Welcome Books™

Children's Press®
A Division of Scholastic Inc.
New York / Toronto / London / Auckland / Sydney
Mexico City / New Delhi / Hong Kong
Danbury, Connecticut

Photo Credits: Cover © Eyewire; pp. 11, 21 (top right) © Gary W. Carter/Corbis; all other photos by Maura B. McConnell
Contributing Editors: Shira Laskin and Jennifer Silate
Book Design: Michael DeLisio

Library of Congress Cataloging-in-Publication Data

Hill, Mary, 1977-
    Let's go to a park / by Mary Hill.
    p. cm. — (Weekend fun)
    ISBN 0-516-23998-8 (lib. bdg.) — ISBN 0-516-25918-0 (pbk.)
    1. Parks—Juvenile literature. 2. Parks—Recreational use—Juvenile
literature. I. Title. II. Series.

    SB481.3H55 2003
    363.6'8— dc22

                                                            2003014453

Contents

My name is David.

After breakfast, my parents and I are going to the **park**.

5

We bring a ball and food
to the park.

Mom packs them in
her bag.

When we get to the park, we go for a walk.

We walk on a **trail**.

9

Look!

There is a pretty red bird.

There is a **playground** in the park.

After our walk, I play on it.

13

I like to **swing** on the swings.

I can swing high.

It is time for lunch.

We eat at a **picnic table**.

After lunch, we play catch.

I throw the ball to Dad.

18

19

We had a lot of fun at the park today!

21

New Words

park (**park**) a place where people go to walk or rest or play games and have fun outside

picnic table (**pik**-nik **tay**-buhl) a table that is used for eating outdoors

playground (**play**-ground) a place where you can play outside

swing (**swing**) a ride on which you can sit and move back and forth

trail (**trayl**) a track or path for people to follow, especially in the woods

To Find Out More

Books
Signs at the Park
by Mary Hill
Scholastic Library Publishing

Yellowstone National Park
by David Petersen
Children's Press

Web Site
Yellowstone National Park: Just for Kids!
http://www.nps.gov/yell/kidstuff/
Take a quiz, print a picture to color, and play games about
Yellowstone National Park on this Web site.

Index

About the Author
Mary Hill has written many books for children. For fun on the weekends, she likes to go sailing.

Reading Consultants
Kris Flynn, Coordinator, Small School District Literacy, The San Diego County Office of Education

Shelly Forys, Certified Reading Recovery Specialist, W.J. Zahnow Elementary School, Waterloo, IL

Paulette Mansell, Certified Reading Recovery Specialist, and Early Literacy Consultant, TX

24